SAAS

Diese Buchreihe stellt Band für Band die Bauwerke von ausgewählten jüngeren Schweizer Architekturschaffenden vor, deren Arbeiten durch besondere Qualität überzeugen. Seit 2004 kuratieren wir die Reihe *Anthologie* in Form einfacher Werkdokumentationen. Sie ist vergleichbar mit der «Blütenlese», wie sie in der Literatur für eine Textsammlung vorgenommen wird. Es liegt in der Natur des Architektenberufs, dass die Erstlingswerke meist kleinere, übersichtliche Bauaufgaben sind. Sie sind eine Art Fingerübung, mit der junge Architekturschaffende das Erlernte anwenden und ihr architektonisches Sensorium erproben und entfalten können. Begabung und Leidenschaft für das Metier lassen sich dabei früh in voller Deutlichkeit und Frische erkennen. So stecken in jedem der kleinen und grossen Projekte inspirierte Grundgedanken und Vorstellungen, die spielerisch und zugleich perfekt in architektonische Bilder, Formen und Räume umgesetzt werden. Immer wieder wird mir dadurch bewusst, dass in der Architektur wie in anderen Kunstformen die Bilder und Ideen, die hinter einem Werk stehen, das Wesentliche sind. Es mag diese Intuition sein, die Kunstschaffende haben, die über ihr Werk wie ein Funke auf die Betrachtenden überspringt, so wie es der italienische Philosoph Benedetto Croce in seinen Schriften eindringlich beschrieben hat.

Heinz Wirz
Verleger

Each volume in this series presents buildings by selected young Swiss architects whose works impress with exceptional quality. Since 2004, we have been curating the *Anthologie* series by simply documenting their oeuvre. The series can be compared to a literary anthology presenting a collection of selected texts. It is in the nature of the architectural profession that early works are mostly small, limited building tasks. They are a kind of five-finger exercise in which the young architects apply what they have learnt, as well as testing and developing their architectural instincts. Talent and a passion for the profession can be seen at an early stage in all of its clarity and freshness. Each project, be it large or small, contains an inspired underlying concept and ideas that are playfully and consummately implemented as architectural images, forms and spaces. Thus, I am regularly reminded that in architecture, as in other art forms, the essence of a piece of work is formed by the images and ideas upon which it is based. Perhaps this is the same intuition described so vividly by the Italian philosopher Benedetto Croce, one that is absorbed by the artist and flies like a spark via the work to the viewer.

Heinz Wirz
Publisher

SAAS

QUART

Die architektonische Produktion von SAAS entspringt weder der Laune eines Autors, noch ist sie ein modisches Outfit. Sie folgt daher auch keinem Rezept und ist kein Dienstleistungsprodukt. Das wäre viel zu leichtfertig und der Verantwortung, die wir als Architekten tragen, unwürdig. Bei dem Versuch, das grelle Licht unserer Zeit zu neutralisieren, tasten wir uns auf der Suche nach einigen unzeitgemässen Überlegungen durch die Dunkelheit und akzeptieren die daraus resultierende Phasenverschiebung. Dies setzt eine Freude am Spiel voraus, das eine gewisse Distanz schafft und es uns ermöglicht, die Vergangenheit zu beleuchten, sie zur Vernunft zu bringen und auf die Gegenwart zu reagieren. Man muss aber auch in der Lage sein, daraus ein kohärentes und schönes Werk zu generieren. Das ist nicht einfach. Vor allem nicht in einer Disziplin, die nur durch äussere Anreize in Gang gesetzt und gerechtfertigt werden kann – durch die Kundschaft, seien es Einzelpersonen oder Institutionen, und durch die Geografie. Wir praktizieren keine eigenständige Disziplin und sind auch keine Künstler. Es ist also ein chaotisches Abenteuer, dessen Ziel es ist, eine klare, engagierte und schöne Architektur zu erreichen, die keine Signatur, sondern eine Haltung impliziert.

PRACTICE

The architectural production of SAAS neither stems from the mood of an author, nor is it a trend outfit. It therefore follows no recipe and is no service-provider's product. That would be far too reckless and unworthy of the responsibility we bear as architects. In an attempt to neutralise the glaring lights of our times, we feel our way through the dark in search of a few outmoded considerations and accept the resulting phase shift. This presupposes a pleasure in the game that a certain distance creates, allowing us to shed light on the past, instil a certain rationalism and react to the present day. However, we must also be able to generate a coherent and beautiful work out of it, which is not easy. Especially not in a field that is only initiated by external impetus, be it the client, individuals or institutions, or the geography. We do not practise an autonomous discipline, nor are we artists. It is therefore a chaotic adventure aimed at achieving clear, committed and beautiful architecture that implies a stance rather than a signature.

2011–2013
Verzinkte Stahlschrauben,
Walliser Lärche, Betonrohre,
Goldpulver. Mit Ateliers
ABX, Michael Meier

2011–2013
Galvanised steel screws,
Valais larch, concrete
pipes, gold powder.
With Ateliers ABX,
Michael Meier

VOGELWARTE PLANFONDS, BERNEX

Die Rhône fliesst nach Westen, aus der Stadt Genf in Richtung Marseille. Der Fluss und sein Ufer wurden im Laufe des 20. Jahrhunderts mehrmals und auf verschiedene Weisen missbraucht. Die Plattform ist Teil eines Projekts zur Renaturierung der Flussufer. Lagunen und Schilfgebiete wurden kreiert, um die Schwankungen des Wasserspiegels abzuschwächen. Fische und vor allem Vögel finden hier kleine Oasen, um sich zu ernähren, auszuruhen und zu brüten. Die Plattform wirkt wie eine visuelle Schutzpalisade für die ankommende Besucherschaft. Vom Ufer losgelöst und auf dünnen Beinen stehend (Schraubfundamente), kann sie jederzeit abmontiert werden, ohne Spuren zu hinterlassen. Einige *objets trouvés*, die im Industriegebiet am anderen Ufer gesammelt wurden, bilden die wenigen Stufen, über die man an Bord gehen kann.

PLANFONDS ORNITHOLOGICAL STATION, BERNEX

The Rhône flows west from the city of Geneva towards Marseille. During the 20th century, the river and its banks were poorly managed and repeatedly damaged. The platform is part of a project to renaturise the river banks. Lagoons and reed areas were created to mitigate the effects of fluctuating water levels. Fish and especially birds find small oases there, where they can feed, rest and breed. The platform has the visual effect of a shielding palisade for the arriving visitors. Released from the bank and standing on thin legs (earthscrew foundations), it can be dismantled at any time without leaving any traces. The few steps leading up to the platform consist of *objets trouvés* collected from the industrial estate on the opposite bank.

5m

2012–2015
Betonstufen (Upcycling),
Walliser Lärche,
Zementfliesen. Mit EDMS,
Michael Meier

2012–2015
Concrete steps (upcycling),
Valais larch, cement tiles.
With EDMS, Michael Meier

PAVILLON, JUSSY

Auf dem ehemaligen Betonparkplatz wurde ein Ziergarten angelegt. Das Erd-geschoss ist nun freier und grosszügiger, ein Fenster zum neuen Garten erhellt die durchgehende Küche. Der Wunsch der Bauherrschaft, eine Garage in den Garten zu bauen, wurde erfüllt. Mit dem Haus verbunden, zeichnet sie ihn räumlich nach. Die Wände sind beweglich, die Materialen zeugen vom länd-lichen Kontext, die Kannelierung verleiht der Garage eine Orientierung zum Garten und gleichzeitig ein kulturelles Gesicht. Abendessen, Geburtstags-feiern und Sonntagsgrillen im Sommer; Bienenstöcke, Atelier und Fahrräder im Winter. Die Garage ist zu einer Art Lustpavillon avanciert, wird nie als Garage genutzt.

PAVILION, JUSSY

An ornamental garden has been laid out on the former concrete car park. The ground floor of the house has been remodelled and made more generous, while a window facing the new garden brightens up the through-kitchen. The client's wish to build a garage was fulfilled. Con-nected to the house, together they spatially define the garden. The walls can be opened completely, the materials reflect the rural context, and the fluting of the columns on one side gives the garage both its orienta-tion towards the garden and the image of a cultural artefact. Dining, birthday celebrations and Sunday barbecues in the summer; beehives, a studio and bicycles in the winter. The garage has advanced to a kind of leisure pavilion and is never used as a garage.

5 m

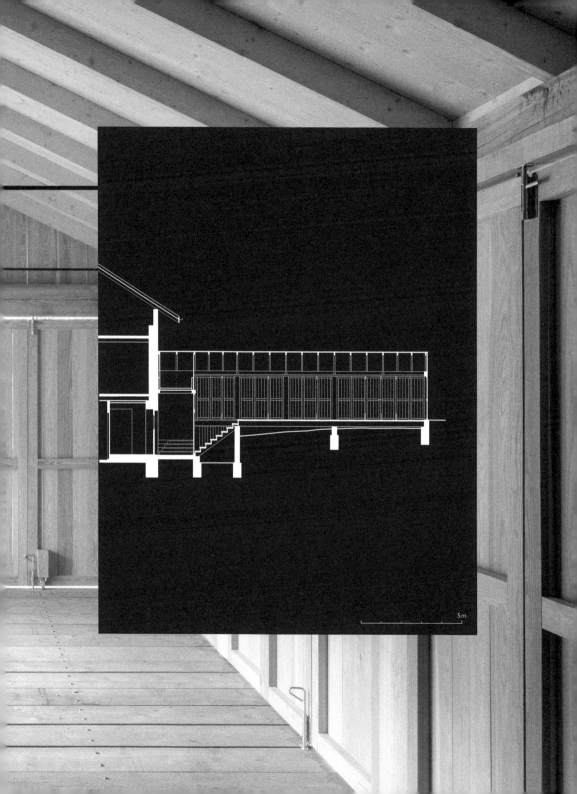

5 m

2015–2017 (hängig)
Vorhandene Steinmauern,
Cortenstahl, Vetiver-
wurzeln, Farbe.
Mit Jean-Christophe
Grosso, Michael Meier

**2015–2017 (pending)
Existing stone walls,
Corten steel, vetiver
roots, paint. With
Jean-Christophe
Grosso, Michael Meier**

KAPELLE, DAMASSINE, HAITI

Das Karibische Meer ist in Sichtweite. Von der Küste aus sind es vier Stunden zu Fuss. Oben auf dem Pass kreuzen sich alle Wege. Jeden Samstag findet da ein Markt statt. Die Einheimischen laufen dort hin, ihre Ladung auf dem Rücken. Sie kommen an, breiten ihre Fracht auf dem Boden aus, verkaufen und kaufen. Am Sonntag wird oft gesungen und musiziert, aber der Platz in der Kapelle ist zu klein an jenen Tagen, an denen der Priester seine Zeremonie abhält. Der Entwurf behält die bestehenden Steinmauern bei, die als Gegengewicht zur reissenden Kraft der Hurrikans dienen. Ihre von der Sonne geschützte Masse dient als kühlende Quelle. Die Profile der tragenden Struktur und die Wände bestehen aus Cortenstahl. Jedes Bauelement darf maximal 40 Kilogramm wiegen: die Last, die zwei Personen vier Stunden lang tragen können.

CHAPEL, DAMASSINE, HAITI

The Caribbean Sea is within sight, a four-hour walk away. All paths cross high upon the pass. A market is held there every Saturday. The locals walk to it with their loads on their backs. They arrive, spread their wares out on the ground, buy and sell. On Sunday, there is singing and music, but the space in the chapel is too limited on days when the priest holds his ceremonies. The project keeps the existing stone walls that serve as a counterweight to the raging force of the hurricanes. Their sun-shielded mass serves as a source of cooling. The profiles of the load-bearing structure and the walls are made of Corten sheet steel. Each building element can only weigh a maximum of 40 kilograms: the load that two people can carry for four hours.

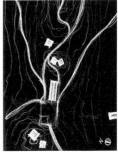

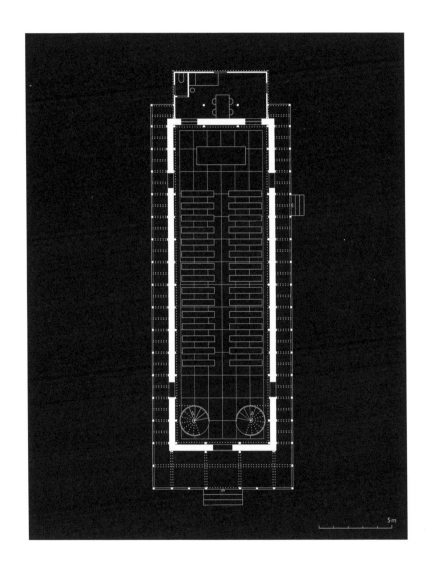

5m

2015–2018
Vorhandene doppelte
Ziegelmauern, Hourdis-
decken, monolithisches
Mauerwerk, Dämmputz
mit Kieselgel, Rouge du
Languedoc

**2015–2018
Existing double brick
walls, hollow-gauged
ceilings, monolithic
masonry, insulating
plaster with silica gel,
Rouge du Languedoc**

UMBAU/ANBAU EINFAMILIENHAUS, CHEXBRES

Das kleine Haus aus den 1950er Jahren hat eine gesunde Substanz – spartanisch, trocken, aber in gutem Zustand. Die Erweiterung des Volumens nach Osten brachte eine typologische Veränderung mit sich: Die neu gewonnene Länge verlangte nach einer Verlegung des Haupteingangs. So wurde das kleine Haus in eine Villa umgewandelt. Die neue Eingangshalle trennt den privaten Bereich von den Gemeinschaftsräumen, der Küche und dem Wohn-/Esszimmer. Der Anbau nutzt die Topografie geschickt aus: Durch die Variation im Terrain wird im Wohnzimmer eine aussergewöhnliche Deckenhöhe erreicht. Zwei symmetrische Treppen nutzen die alten Fensteröffnungen und verbinden Flur, Küche und Wohnzimmer zu einem räumlich vielseitigen Ensemble.

SINGLE-FAMILY HOME CONVERSION/EXTENSION, CHEXBRES

The small 1950s house has a healthy structure: spartan, lean, but in a good condition. The extension towards the east brought about a typological change: the newly gained length required the main entrance to be moved. Thus the small house was transformed into a villa. The new entrance hall divides the private area from the communal rooms, the kitchen and the living/dining room. The extension cleverly exploits the topography, using the variation in the terrain to create an exceptional ceiling height in the living room. Two symmetrical stairs use the old window apertures and connect the hall, kitchen and living room to create a diverse spatial ensemble.

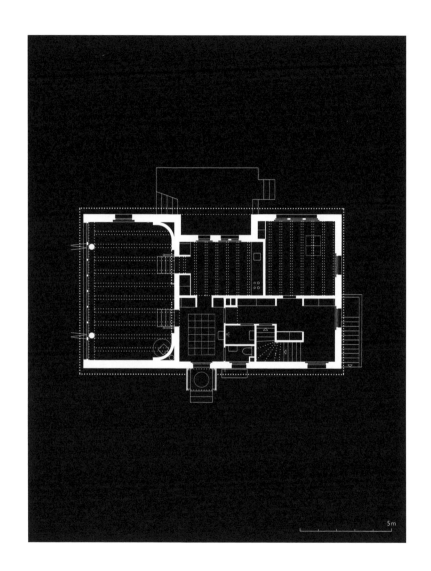

5m

2017–2018 (hängig)
Cortenstahl, Farbe,
lokale Energie. Mit Raphaël
Dunant, Christian Portmann

**2017–2018 (pending)
Corten steel, paint,
local energy. With
Raphaël Dunant,
Christian Portmann**

HANDWERKSPARK, MOREAU, HAITI

In Haiti wächst alles: Kaffee, Kakao, Mangos, Papayas, Maniok, Erbsen aller Art.
Der Handwerkspark bietet den Bäuerinnen und Bauern die nötige Infrastruktur, um aus Rohprodukten höherwertige Verkaufsprodukte herzustellen. Dies
ermöglicht ihnen auch, den Zwischenhandel zu überspringen, der die grösste
Gewinnspanne einstreicht, ohne etwas zu riskieren. Das u-förmige Gebäude
erstreckt sich der Topografie folgend nach unten in Richtung des Flussbetts.
Eine kollektive Galerie ermöglicht es der Besucher- und Arbeiterschaft, sich
geschützt vor Sonne und Regen zu bewegen. Entlang der Galerie und der Topografie wird das Regenwasser in den Garten geleitet, wo sich die Gemeinschaftsküche, der Speisesaal und ein kleines Haus befinden.

CRAFTS PARK, MOREAU, HAITI

**Everything grows in Haiti: coffee, cocoa, mangoes, papayas, cassavas and
all kinds of peas. The Crafts Park offers the farmers the necessary infrastructure to turn raw materials into high-quality consumer products.
It also enables them to do without middlemen, who make the largest
profits without any risk. The U-shaped building stretches down along the
contours of the topography towards the riverbed. A collective gallery
protects visitors and workers from the sun and rain as they move around.
Rainwater is guided along the gallery and the terrain into a pound in the
garden, where the communal kitchen, the dining room and a small guesthouse are located.**

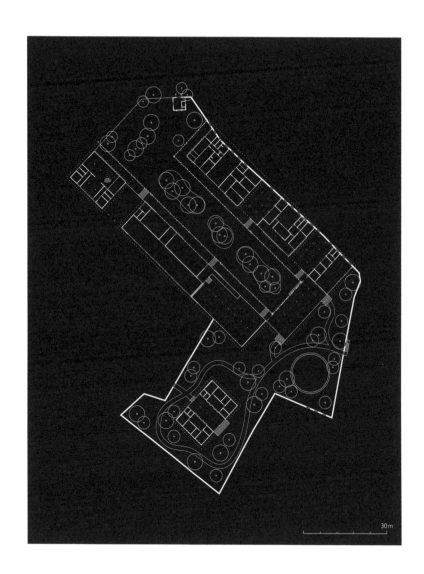

30 m

2015–2019
Freiburger Fichtenholz,
Beton, Stahlblech

2015–2019
**Fribourg spruce,
concrete, sheet steel**

VILLA FÜR ZWEI FAMILIEN, ORMONT-DESSUS

So wie sich die Villen des venezianischen Landadels im 16. Jahrhundert rund um Vicenza durchsetzten, so eroberte der gehobene Tourismus aus aller Welt die Alpen im 20. Jahrhundert. Und das mit einer solchen Wucht, dass die örtliche Bauordnung die Typologie des Chalets als Standard anerkannte. *Exit* leichte, zweistöckige Seitengalerien auf dünnen Stelzen, *exit* Veranden: Die Bauordnung, deren ausdrücklicher Auftrag es ist, das Ortsbild und seine Identität zu schützen, verbietet Verweise auf die vernakuläre Architektur. Das wurde ernst genommen. Das fast schon klassische Doppelchalet bietet Wohnraum für zwei Familien. Die kollektive Eingangshalle gewährt Zugang zu den beiden Einheiten, deren Bewohnerschaften sich danach nicht mehr begegnen.

VILLA FOR TWO FAMILIES, ORMONT-DESSUS

Just as villas conquered the Venetian countryside around Vicenza in the 16th century, so did exclusive Alpine tourism from all around the world take hold in the 20th century. It became so forceful that the local building regulations recognised the typology of the chalet as standard. *Exit* lightness and two-storey lateral galleries on narrow stilts, *exit* verandas: the building regulations, whose explicit task is to protect the local character and identity, prohibit references to vernacular architecture. This was taken seriously. The almost classic double chalet offers housing for two families. The common entrance hall provides access to both units, after which the inhabitants no longer encounter each other.

5 m

2019–2020
Stahlprofile (wieder-
verwendet), thermische
Vorhänge, Gartenfliesen,
Pflanzen. Selbstbau, mit
Cloé Gattigo

2019–2020
Re-used steel structure,
insulating curtains, garden
tiles, plants. Self-build,
with Cloé Gattigo

UMBAU FABRIKGEBÄUDE, CAROUGE

Das solide Betonskelett der alten Brauerei schafft in Kombination mit der teil-
weise vorhandenen, aber angepassten Stahlkonstruktion abwechslungsreiche
und spannende Räume. Die unterschiedlichen Raumhöhen und -ausrichtungen,
gekoppelt mit beweglichen Architekturelementen, ermöglichen eine Feinab-
stimmung des Raumklimas. Je nach Jahreszeit, Temperatur und Nutzung können unterschiedliche Raumkonfigurationen entstehen. Wohnen und Arbeiten
sind eng miteinander verbunden und teilen sich einen Teil der Infrastruktur
(gemeinsame Nutzung der Küche). Thermovorhänge verleihen den Räumen
zusätzliche Präzision, je nach Nutzung, Temperatur oder Rückzugsbedürfnis.

FACTORY BUILDING CONVERSION, CAROUGE

The solid concrete skeleton of the old brewery combines with the par-
tially existent, yet adapted steel structure to produce varying room
heights and exciting spaces. This spatial arrangement and the movable
architectural elements allow the room climate to be sensitively adjusted.
Depending on the season, temperature and use, different room configur-
ations can be achieved. Living and working are closely linked and share
part of the infrastructure (along with the use of the kitchen). Insulating curtains give the rooms additional precision, depending on the use,
temperature and any need for retreat.

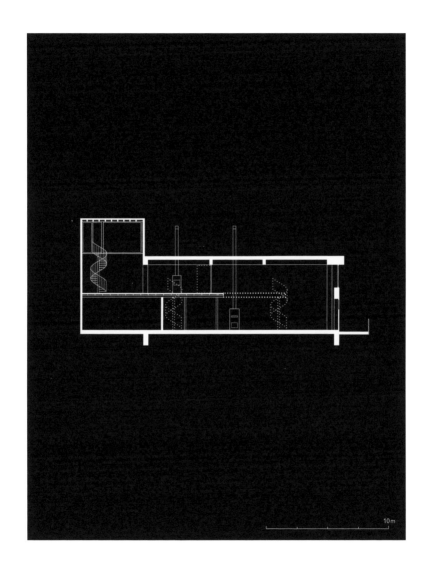

10m

2018–2023
Sandsteinplatten,
Terrakottafliesen,
massives Eichenparkett
(wiederverwendet),
massive Fichtendielen.
Mit Christ&Gantenbein

**2018–2023
Sandstone slabs,
terracotta tiles, solid
re-used oak parquet,
solid spruce floorboards.
With Christ&Gantenbein**

* Frei nach Jenny Keller,
«Architekturführer –
Umbau Musee international
de la Reforme», in: *Werk,
Bauen + Wohnen*, Nr. 4, 2023,
S. 25.
*** Loosely based on
Jenny Keller: "Architektur-
führer – Umbau Musee
international de la
Reforme". In: *werk, bauen +
wohnen*, No. 4, 2023, p. 25.**

UMBAU INTERNATIONALES MUSEUM DER REFORMATION, GENF

Nur eine schmale Gasse trennt das ehemalige Hôtel particulier von der goti-schen Kathedrale. Die Gäste betraten das Palais einst nicht über den Hof des u-förmigen Gebäudes – das war der Bewohnerschaft vorbehalten –, sondern über den Eingang am Platz, wo die Kutschen vorfahren konnten. 30 Jahre nach der Erbauung im Jahr 1721 sorgten drei Geschosswohnungen in den schwer zu heizenden Gemäuern für eine bessere Wirtschaftlichkeit der Immobilie; das Wohnhaus wurde künftig über die Seitengasse betreten. Nochmals 250 Jahre später (2005) zog das Museum im Erdgeschoss ein. Durch gezielte Eingriffe und Sanierungen reanimieren die Architekten die ursprüngliche Typologie. Stein-platten statt Parkettboden markieren den Eingangsbereich, der erneut zur Ein-gangshalle wird und sich sich wieder «verkehrt herum» zum Platz der Kathed-rale öffnet.*

INTERNATIONAL MUSEUM OF THE REFORMATION CONVERSION, GENEVA

Only a narrow alley separates the former Hôtel particulier from the Gothic cathedral. In the past, guests did not enter the palais via the courtyard of the U-shaped building, since that was reserved for the resi-dents. Instead, guests used an entrance from the square, where coaches could drive by. 30 years after its construction in 1721, three single-storey apartments in the building, which had previously been difficult to heat, improved its economy; the residential building was subsequently entered via the side street. Another 250 years later (2005), the museum moved in on its ground floor. The architects used targeted interventions and refurbishing measures to reanimate the original typology. Stone slabs rather than parquet flooring mark the entrance area, which once again becomes the entrance hall, again opening up "back-to-front" towards the cathedral square.*

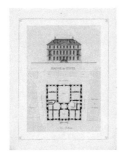

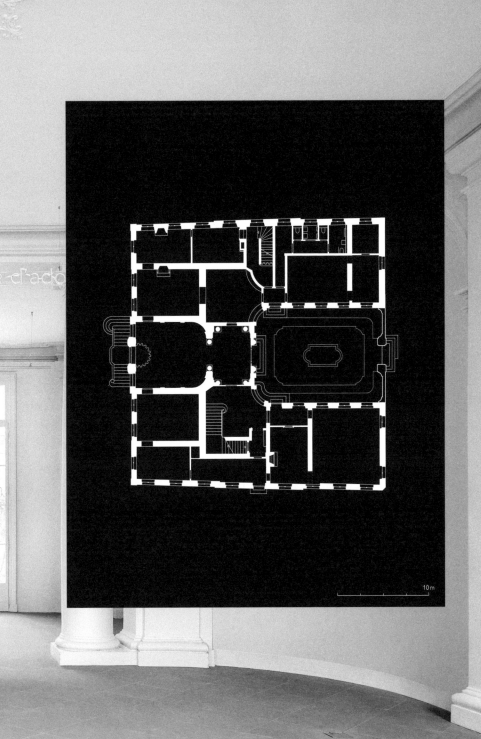

10 m

2019–2023 (laufend)
Aushubmaterial,
Lehmsteine, Beton, Stahl.
Mit ADR, EDMS

2019–2023 (ongoing)
Excavation material,
clay stone, concrete,
steel. With ADR, EDMS

ALTE ZIEGELEI, BARDONNEX

Eine Schicht aus rotbraunem Lehm, versteckt unter der grünen Landschaft. 1946 wird die Ziegelei von Bardonnex gegründet. Der Ofen verbraucht täglich 2000 Liter Schweröl. Doch unter dem Lehm befindet sich etwas noch Wertvolleres: Kies und Sand, die für Beton abgebaut werden können. Die Ziegelei wird 2020 stillgelegt. Umnutzung der Hallen? Aufgrund der heutigen Normen unmöglich. Recycling? Alle Wege und Materialbörsen werden bemüht – ohne Erfolg. Also Abriss. Das künstliche Plateau aus Ziegelresten ist nach Genfer Vorschriften ein kontaminierter Standort. Das gilt auch für das Abbruchmaterial der Ziegelei. Statt auf der Deponie zu landen, wird es zum Rohstoff des neuen Projekts: Kies und Sand aus dem Aushub werden dem Beton beigemischt. Lehmziegel aus Aushubmaterial, vermischt mit Abbruchmaterial und Lehm aus der Mine, bilden die Fassade.

OLD BRICKWORKS, BARDONNEX

A layer of reddish-brown clay hidden beneath the green landscape. The Bardonnex brickyard was founded in 1946. The kiln consumes 2,000 litres of heavy oil every day. But something even more valuable lies beneath the clay: gravel and sand, which are quarried for concrete. The brickworks closed in 2020. Convert the halls? Impossible by today's standards. Recycling? All material exchanges were tried – without success. So demolition. The artificial plateau of brick remains is a contaminated site according to Geneva regulations. This also applies to the demolition material from the brickyard. Instead of ending up in a landfill, it became the raw material for the new project: gravel and sand from the excavated material were added to the concrete. Clay bricks from excavated material, mixed with demolition material and clay from the pit, form the façade.

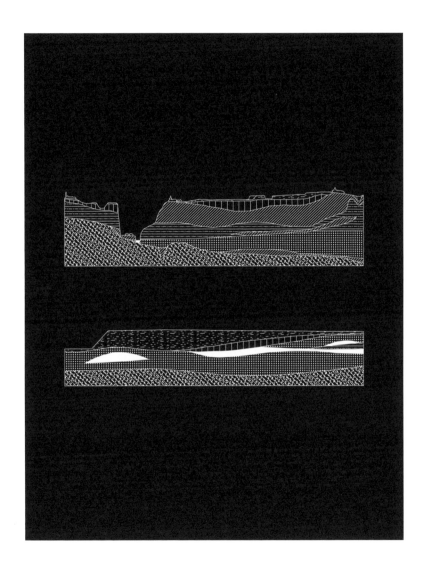

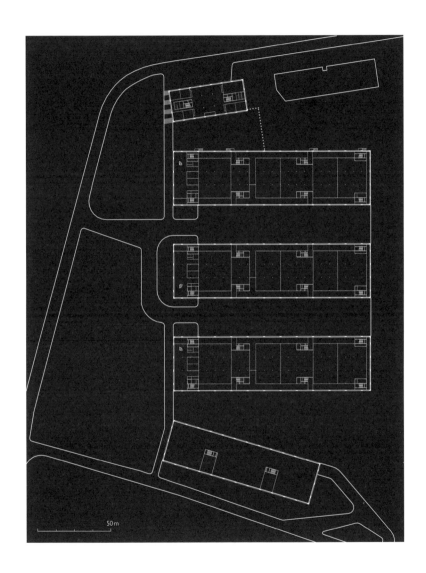

50m

In medias res, ohne Fluchtmöglichkeit. Architektur ist in der Tat eine Form der Reflexion über die Stadt, die bereits da ist; über das Leben, das sich bereits in ihr abspielt. Die Stadt könnte als das Zufällige, Besondere gesehen werden. Und die Architektur als das Rationale und Universelle. Es ist durchaus möglich, dass die Architektur zunächst einige unmittelbare Probleme der Stadt ignorieren muss; als ideales Modell mit öffentlichem Charakter kann sie nicht alles lösen, was spezifisch und individuell ist. Sie braucht eine gewisse Distanz zur Gegenwart: ein Schritt weg vom Fluss der Ereignisse, mit dem Ziel, sich Raum zu schaffen; Raum zum Manövrieren und Abstrahieren, um aus der besonderen Realität heraus das Kollektive, das Zeitgenössische zu erreichen. Also die Stadt als chaotisches Produkt von idealen, politischen, sozialen und architektonischen Modellen.

THE CITY – EVERYWHERE

In medias res, without any means of escape. Architecture is indeed a form of reflection on the city that is already there, and on the life that is already happening in it. The city could be regarded as arbitrary and specific, and architecture as rational and universal. It is certainly possible that architecture must initially ignore a number of the city's immediate problems; as an ideal model with a public character, it cannot solve everything that is specific and individual. It requires a certain distance from the present, stepping away from the flow of events, with the aim of creating space; leeway to manoeuvre and abstract, to achieve the collective, the contemporary out of the specific reality. In other words, regarding the city as the chaotic product of ideal, political, social and architectural models.

WERKVERZEICHNIS
Auswahl Bauten, Projekte und Wettbewerbe

2012	Ideenwettbewerb Cardinal Bluefactory, Fribourg (5. Preis)
2013	Machbarkeitstudie Nationaler Innovationspark, Biel (mit BASK)
	Vogelwarte Planfonds, Bernex (mit Ateliers ABX, Michael Meier)
2014	Wettbewerb Opération les Vernets, Genf (mit MS Bern, EDMS, Michael Meier; Finalist)
	Wettbewerb Genève – Ville et Champs, Genf (mit Michael Jakob, Romain Legros, Michael Meier; 1. Preis)
	Parallelstudie im selektiven Verfahren Stiftung Clair-Vivre, Jussy (mit Michael Meier; 2. Preis)
	Wettbewerb Ancien Manège, Genf (mit EDMS, Michael Meier; 2. Preis)
	Parallelstudie in Auswahlverfahren PAV Etoile, Genf (mit Baukuh, LIST)
2015	Pavillon, Jussy (mit EDMS, Michael Meier)
	Umbau einer Arztpraxis, Lausanne (mit Michael Meier)
	Projekt für den Umbau einer Kappelle, Damassine, Haiti (mit Jean-Christophe Grosso, Michael Meier)
2016	Wettbewerb Projet Grand Saconnex, Grand Saconnex (mit Atelier +, MS Bern, EDMS, Michael Meier; 3. Preis, Ankauf)
2017	Wettbewerb Swiss Art Awards, Basel (mit Michael Meier; Finalist)
	Projekt für einen Industrie- und Handwerkspark, Moreau, Haiti (mit Raphaël Dunant, Christian Portmann)
2018	Umbau/Anbau Einfamilienhaus, Chexbres
	Umbau Bauernhof, Correvon
	Wettbewerb Umbau und Erweiterung ITU, Genf (mit Léonie Zelger; Finalist)
	Einfamilienhaus, Camp Perrin, Haiti
2019	Villa für zwei Familien, Ormont-Dessus
	Verdichtungsstudie für das Internationale Komitee vom Roten Kreuz, Genf (mit EDMS)

LIST OF WORKS
Selection of buildings, projects and competitions

2012	Competition for ideas, Fribourg (5th Prize)
2013	Feasibility study, National Innovation Park, Biel (with BASK)
	Planfonds Ornithological Station, Bernex (with Ateliers ABX, Michael Meier)
2014	Competition, Opération les Vernets, Geneva (with MS Bern, EDMS, Michael Meier; Finalist)
	Competition, Genève – Ville et Champs, Geneva (with Michael Jakob, Romain Legros, Michael Meier; 1st Prize)
	Parallel study in a selective process, Clair-Vivre Foundation, Jussy (with Michael Meier; 2nd Prize)
	Competition, Ancien Manège, Geneva (with MEDMS, Michael Meier; 2nd Prize)
	Parallel study in a selective process, PAV Etoile, Geneva (with Baukuh, LIST)
2015	Pavilion, Jussy (with EDMS, Michael Meier)
	Conversion, medical practice, Lausanne (with Michael Meier)
	Chapel conversion design, Damassine, Haiti (with Jean-Christophe Grosso, Michael Meier)
2016	Competition, Projet Grand Saconnex, Grand Saconnex (with Atelier +, MS Bern, EDMS, Michael Meier; 3rd Prize, purchase)
2017	Competition, Swiss Art Awards, Basel (with Michael Meier; Finalist)
	Design, Crafts Park, Moreau, Haiti (with Raphaël Dunant, Christian Portmann)
2018	Conversion/extension, single-family home, Chexbres
	Conversion, farm, Correvon
	Competition, conversion and extension, ITU, Geneva (with Léonie Zelger; Finalist)
	Single-family home, Camp Perrin, Haiti
2019	Villa for two families, Ormont-Dessus
	Densification study, International Committee of the Red Cross, Geneva (with EDMS)

2020	Studie Umwandlung Raffinerie, Monthey (mit Atelier +)
	Wettbewerb Platztor Universität St. Gallen, St. Gallen
	(mit Christian Portmann)
	Umbau Fabrikgebäude, Carouge (mit Cloé Gattigo)
	Studie im selektiven Verfahren Visions prospectives
	pour le Grand Genève, Genf (mit Baukuh,
	Stefano Boeri, Michel Desvigne)
	Wettbewerb Goutte St-Mathieu (mit Atelier +, DUO)
2021	Wettbewerb Strategisches Freiraumkonzept und
	Regelwerk Inselspital, Bern (mit DUO, Panorama AG;
	1. Preis)
	Leitbild Umwandlung einer alten Ziegelei, Bardonnex
	(mit ADR, EDMS)
	Wettbewerb Platforme 10, Lausanne (mit Jonas Løland)
	Wettbewerb Entwicklung Gaswerkareal und
	Brückenkopf West, Bern (mit Atelier +, YellowOffice)
2022	Wettbewerb Abbaye de St-Maurice (mit Schnetzer
	Puskas)
	Wettbewerb Campus EDHEA, Sierre (mit Schnetzer
	Puskas, YellowOffice)
	Wettbewerb Centre Archives et Patrimoine,
	La Chaux-de-Fonds (mit EDMS; 2. Preis)
2023	Umbau Internationales Museum der Reformation, Genf
	(mit Christ&Gantenbein)
	Wettbewerb Nouvelle Ecole Professionnelle, Payerne
	(mit MS Bern, Schnetzer Puskas; 6. Preis)

Laufende Projekte:
Wohngebäude für 18 Wohnungen, Jussy
Sortieranlage, Bardonnex
Fünf industrielle Gebäude, Bardonnex

2020	Study, refinery conversion, Monthey (with Atelier +) Competition, Platztor, University of St. Gallen, St. Gallen (with Christian Portmann) Conversion, factory building, Carouge (with Cloé Gattigo) Study in a selective process, Visions prospectives pour le Grand Genève, Geneva (with Baukuh, Stefano Boeri, Michel Desvigne) Competition, Goutte St-Mathieu (with Atelier +, DUO)
2021	Competition, strategic outdoor spatial concept and regulations, Inselspital, Bern (with DUO, Panorama AG; 1st Prize) Guiding principle, old brickworks conversion, Bardonnex (with ADR, EDMS) Competition, Platforme 10, Lausanne (with Jonas Løland) Competition, development of gasworks estate and Brückenkopf West, Bern (with Atelier +, YellowOffice)
2022	Competition, Abbaye de St-Maurice (with Schnetzer Puskas) Competition, Campus EDHEA, Sierre (with Schnetzer Puskas, YellowOffice) Competition, Centre Archives et Patrimoine, La Chaux-de-Fonds (with EDMS; 2nd Prize)
2023	Conversion, International Museum of the Reformation, Geneva (with Christ&Gantenbein) Competition, Nouvelle Ecole Professionnelle, Payerne (with MS Bern, Schnetzer Puskas; 6th Prize)

Ongoing projects:
Building with 18 apartments, Jussy
Sorting facility, Bardonnex
Five industrial buildings, Bardonnex

GUILLAUME YERSIN

1981	Geboren in Vevey
2000–2003	Studium der Humanmedizin
2003–2009	Architekturstudium an der ETH Zürich und am Tokyo Institute of Technology
2006–2007	Praktikum bei Lacaton & Vassal
	Praktikum bei AMO – Rem Koolhaas
2010–2011	Lehrbeauftragter an der HEAD Genf
2012	Gründung SAAS sàrl
2011–2016	Assistent bei Ass.-Prof. Christ&Gantenbein, ETH Zürich
2021–	Mitglied Bund Schweizer Architektinnen und Architekten (BSA)
2021–2022	Gastprofessur an der Technischen Universität Wien

MITARBEITENDE (EHEMALIG* UND AKTUELL)

Isabelle Cochevelou
Emile Corthay*
Sébastien Le Dortz*
Floriane Fol*
Foucauld Huard
Andrea Ishii
Mona Lecoultre*
Michael Meier*
Elli Moustaka*

GUILLAUME YERSIN

1981	Born in Vevey
2000–2003	Studied Medicine
2003–2009	Studied Architecture at the ETH Zurich and the Tokyo Institute of Technology
2006–2007	Internship at Lacaton & Vassal Internship at AMO – Rem Koolhaas
2010–2011	Lecturer, HEAD Geneva
2012	Founded SAAS sàrl
2011–2016	Assistant to Professors Christ&Gantenbein, ETH Zurich
2021–	Member of the Federation of Swiss Architects (BSA)
2021–2022	Guest Professor, TU Wien

TEAM (PAST* AND PRESENT)

Isabelle Cochevelou
Emile Corthay*
Sébastien Le Dortz*
Floriane Fol*
Foucauld Huard
Andrea Ishii
Mona Lecoultre*
Michael Meier*
Elli Moustaka*

Finanzielle und ideelle Unterstützung

Ein besonderer Dank gilt den Institutionen und Sponsorfirmen, deren finanzielle Unterstützungen wesentlich zum Entstehen dieser Buchreihe beitragen. Ihr kulturelles Engagement ermöglicht ein fruchtbares und freundschaftliches Zusammenwirken von Baukultur und Bauwirtschaft.

Financial and conceptual support

Special thanks to our sponsors and institutions whose financial support has helped us so much with the production of this series of books. Their cultural commitment is a valuable contribution to fruitful and cordial collaboration between the culture and economics of architecture.

ERNST GÖHNER STIFTUNG

Copytrend SA, Genève

EDMS SA, Petit-Lancy

FEUSI CHAUFFAGE, Vésenaz

Gasser Ceramic,
Corcelles-près-Payerne

Graphisoft, Estavayer-le-Lac

Hälg & Cie SA,
Plan-les-Ouates

Karlen Maçonnerie –
Génie civil SA, Blonay

L'Atelier COMTE,
Bardonnex

MAB-Ingénierie SA, Morges

Services Industriels de
Genève, Genève

srg | engineering, Genève

Terrabloc SA, Genève

SAAS
53. Band der Reihe *Anthologie*
Herausgegeben von: Heinz Wirz, Luzern
Konzept: Heinz Wirz; SAAS, Genf
Projektleitung: Quart Verlag, Linus Wirz
Objekttexte: SAAS
Textlektorat deutsch: Miriam Seifert-Waibel, Hamburg
Übersetzung deutsch–englisch: Benjamin Liebelt, Berlin
Fotos: Damien Magat, Genf, S. 40–43; Roman Keller, Zürich, S. 8–17, 44, 45;
SAAS, S. 7, 18, 20–26, 32–38, 50, 52
Renderings: SAAS, Genf, S. 19, 28–30; Valentin Calame / Loïs Bouché, Genf,
S. 46, 48
Redesign: BKVK, Basel – Beat Keusch, Angelina Köpplin-Stützle
Grafische Umsetzung: Quart Verlag Luzern; Manon Mello, Genf
Lithos: Printeria, Luzern
Druck: DZA Druckerei zu Altenburg GmbH

Der Quart Verlag wird vom Bundesamt für Kultur für die Jahre 2021–2024
unterstützt.

SAAS
Volume 53 of the series *Anthologie*
Edited by: Heinz Wirz, Lucerne
Concept: Heinz Wirz; SAAS, Geneva
Project management: Quart Verlag, Linus Wirz
Project descriptions: SAAS
German text editing: Miriam Seifert-Waibel, Hamburg
German–English translation: Benjamin Liebelt, Berlin
Photos: Damien Magat, Geneva, p. 40–43; Roman Keller, Zurich, p. 8–17,
44, 45; SAAS, p. 7, 18, 20–26, 32–38, 50, 52
Renderings: SAAS, Geneva, p. 19, 28–30; Valentin Calame / Loïs Bouché,
Geneva, p. 46, 48
Redesign: BKVK, Basel – Beat Keusch, Angelina Köpplin-Stützle
Graphic design: Quart Verlag Luzern; Manon Mello, Geneva
Lithos: Printeria, Lucerne
Printing: DZA Druckerei zu Altenburg GmbH

Quart Publishers is being supported by the Federal Office of Culture for
the years 2021–2024.

Quart Verlag GmbH
Denkmalstrasse 2, CH-6006 Luzern
books@quart.ch, www.quart.ch

Anthologie
Werkberichte junger Architekturschaffender

Anthologie
Work reports on young architects

*inserted booklet with translation